DALTON EXLEY

IN NATURE IS LIFE

A compelling tribute to the natural world in words and pictures

What would the world be, once bereft
Of wet and wildness? Let them be left
O let them be left, wildness and wet;
Long live the weeds and the wilderness yet.

GERARD MANLEY HOPKINS (1844-1889)

EXLEY
NEW YORK • WATFORD, UK

This anthology represents a labour of love for me, it isn't intended to assume any kind of voice of authority or preach to anyone.
More simply, these words moved me and I hope some of these writings or pictures strike a chord or raise a smile, that's all.
I would like to thank my father, Richard, for taking us to the countryside of so many lands at so early an age, and encouraging a love for (and little fear of) nature. My mother Helen for her continual love, support and trust. My love and thanks go to Clare for everything. I'd like to thank Martin Kerr for helping with my designs, and thanks also to Marion, Paul, Beaker, Ben and Zoe, James and Kath – *Dalton Exley.*

Published simultaneously in 2000 by Exley Publications Ltd in Great Britain and Exley Publications LLC in the USA.

2 4 6 8 10 12 11 9 7 5 3 1

Selection and arrangement copyright © Dalton Exley 2000
The moral right of the author has been asserted.

ISBN 1-86187-087-6

Words and pictures researched and selected by Dalton Exley.
Printed in Italy.

Exley Publications Ltd, 16 Chalk Hill, Watford, Herts WD1 4BN, UK.
Exley Publications LLC, 232 Madison Avenue, Suite 1409, NY10016, USA.

DALTON EXLEY

IN NATURE IS LIFE

EXLEY
NEW YORK • WATFORD, UK

If you try
to think both together

the blackness and the stars
and the close blue sky

it almost seems we move inside the bubble
as if it were a room with a fire
on a very cold night

and that if it burst

the cold would come rushing in
and hurt as much
as your brain can
looking farther and farther past
stars and stars
and black on top of black
until you have to think about something
never ending
and can't.

LAWRENCE COLLINS

The earth is not... a mere fragment of dead history, strata upon strata,
like the leaves of a book, an object for a museum and an antiquarian,
but living poetry like the leaves of a tree, –
not a fossil earth, but a living specimen.

HENRY DAVID THOREAU (1817-1862)

Over all the hilltops

Silence,

Among the treetops

You feel hardly

A breath moving.

The birds fall silent in the woods.

Simply wait! Soon

You too will be silent.

JOHANN WOLFGANG VON GOETHE
(1749-1832)

Dewdrops, let me cleanse

in your brief, sweet waters

These dark hands of life.

BASHO (1644-1694)

QUIETENING THE MIND,
DEEP IN THE FOREST
WATER DRIPS DOWN.

HOSHA

... nature itself means nothing,
says nothing except to the perceiving mind....
Beauty is where it is perceived...
you surely will see... if you are prepared to see it –
if you look for it....

HENRY DAVID THOREAU (1817-1862)

It is only in exceptional moods that we realize
how wonderful are the commonest experiences of life.
It seems to me sometimes that these experiences
have an "inner" side, as well as the outer side we normally perceive.
At such moments one suddenly sees everything with new eyes;
one feels on the brink of some great revelation.
It is as if we caught a glimpse of some incredibly beautiful world
that lies silently about us all the time.

J.W.N. SULLIVAN

JANUARY 7, 1857

... alone in distant woods or fields, in unpretending sproutlands or pastures
tracked by rabbits, even in a bleak and, to most, cheerless day, like this, when a
villager would be thinking of his inn, I come to myself, I once more feel myself
grandly related, and that cold and solitude are friends of mine. I suppose that this
value, in my case, is equivalent to what others get by church-going and prayer. I
come to my solitary woodland walk as the homesick go home. I thus dispose of
the superfluous and see things as they are, grand and beautiful. I have told many
that I walk every day about half the daylight, but I think they do not believe it.
I wish to get the Concord, the Massachusetts, the America, out of my head and
be sane a part of every day.... I wish to forget, a considerable part of every

day, all mean, narrow, trivial men..., and therefore I come out to these solitudes, where the problem of existence is simplified. I get away a mile or two from the town into the stillness and solitude of nature, with rocks, trees, weeds, snow about me. I enter some glade in the woods, perchance, where a few weeds and dry leaves alone lift themselves above the surface of the snow, and it is as if I had come to an open window. I see out and around myself.... This stillness, solitude, wildness of nature is a kind of thoroughwort, or boneset, to my intellect. This is what I go out to seek. It is as if I always met in those places some grand, serene, immortal, infinitely encouraging, though invisible, companion, and walked with him.

HENRY DAVID THOREAU (1817-1862)

Few come to the woods to see how the pine lives and grows and spires, lifting its evergreen arms to the light, to see its perfect success. Most are content to behold it in the shape of many broad boards brought to market, and deem that its true success. The pine is no more lumber than man is, and to be made into boards and houses is no more its true and highest use than the truest use of man is to be cut down and made into manure. A pine cut down, a dead pine, is no more a pine than a dead human carcass is a man. Is it the lumberman who is the friend and lover of the pine, stands nearest to it, and understands its nature best? Is it the tanner or turpentine distiller who posterity will fable was changed into a pine at last? No, no, it is the poet who makes the truest use of the pine, who does not fondle it with an axe, or tickle it with a saw, or stroke it with a plane. It is the poet who loves it as his own shadow in the air, and lets it stand. It is as immortal as I am, and will go to as high a heaven, there to tower above me still. Can he who has only discovered the value of whale-bone and whale-oil be said to have discovered the true uses of the whale? Can he who slays the elephant for ivory be said to have seen the elephant? No, these are petty accidental uses. Just as if a stronger race were to kill us in order to make buttons and flageolets of our bones, and then prate of the usefulness of man. Every creature is better alive than dead, both men and moose and pine-trees, as life is more beautiful than death.

HENRY DAVID THOREAU (1817-1862)

HEIRLOOM

She gave me childhood's flowers,
Heather and wild thyme,
Eyebright and tormentil,
Lichen's mealy cup
Dry on wind-scored stone,
The corbies on the rock,
The rowan by the burn.

Sea-marvels a child beheld
Out in the fisherman's boat,
Fringed pulsing violet
Medusa, sea-gooseberries,
Starfish on the sea-floor
Cowries and rainbow-shells
From pools on a rocky shore,

Gave me her memories,
But kept her last treasure:
'When I was a lass', she said,
'Sitting among the heather,
'Suddenly I saw
'That all the moor was alive!
'I have told no one before'.

That was my mother's tale.
Seventy years had gone
Since she saw the living skein
Of which the world is woven,
And having seen, knew all;
Through long indifferent years
Treasuring the priceless pearl.

KATHLEEN RAINE,
B. 1908

Hills are always more beautiful than stone buildings, you know. Living in a city

is an artificial existence. Lots of people hardly ever feel real soil under their feet,

see plants grow except in flower pots, or get far enough beyond the street light

to catch the enchantment of a night sky studded with stars.

TATANGA MANI OR WALKING BUFFALO, A STONEY INDIAN

... A child said *What is the grass?*...

... And now it seems to me the beautiful uncut hair of graves.

... The smallest sprout shows there is really no death,
And if ever there was it led forward life, and does not wait at
  the end to arrest it,

... This is the grass that grows wherever the land is and the water is,
This is the common air that bathes the globe.

... I believe a leaf of grass is no less than the journey-work of the stars,
... And a mouse is miracle enough to stagger sextillions of infidels.

WALT WHITMAN (1819-1891), FROM "SONG OF MYSELF"

Hast never come to thee an hour,
A sudden gleam divine, precipitating,
  bursting all these bubbles, fashions,
  wealth?
These eager business aims – books,
  politics, art, amours,
To utter nothingness?

WALT WHITMAN (1819-1891)

Sometimes, when a bird cries out,
Or the wind sweeps through a tree,
Or a dog howls in a far off farm,
I hold still and listen a long time.

My soul turns and goes back to the place
Where, a thousand forgotten years ago,
The bird and the blowing wind
Were like me, and were my brothers.

My soul turns into a tree,
And an animal, and a cloud bank.
Then changed and odd it comes home
And asks me questions. What should I reply?

HERMANN HESSE (1877-1962)

A land not mine, still
forever memorable,
the waters of its ocean
chill and fresh.

Sand on the bottom whiter than chalk,
and the air drunk, like wine,
late sun lays bare
the rosy limbs of the pinetrees.

Sunset in the ethereal waves:
I cannot tell if the day
is ending, or the world, or if
the secret of secrets is inside me again.

ANNA AKHMATOVA
(1889-1966)

VEGETATION

O never harm the dreaming world,
The world of green, the world of leaves,
But let its million palms unfold
The adoration of the trees.

It is a love in darkness wrought
Obedient to the unseen sun,
Longer than memory, a thought
Deeper than the graves of time.

The turning spindles of the cells
Weave a slow forest over space,
The dance of love, creation....

KATHLEEN RAINE, B. 1908

WILD GEESE

You do not have to be good.

You do not have to walk on your knees

for a hundred miles through the desert, repenting.

You only have to let the soft animal of your body

  love what it loves.

Tell me about despair, yours, and I will tell you mine.

Meanwhile the world goes on.

Meanwhile the sun and the clear pebbles of the rain

are moving across the landscapes,

over the prairies and the deep trees,

the mountains and the rivers.

Meanwhile the wild geese, high in the clean blue air,

are heading home again.

Whoever you are, no matter how lonely,

the world offers itself to your imagination,

calls to you like the wild geese, harsh and exciting —

over and over announcing your place

in the family of things.

MARY OLIVER, B.1935

THE PEACE OF WILD THINGS

When despair for the world grows in me
and I wake in the night at the least sound
in fear of what my life and my children's lives may be,
I go and lie down where the wood drake
rests in his beauty on the water, and the great heron feeds.
I come into the peace of wild things
who do not tax their lives with forethought
of grief. I come into the presence of still water.
And I feel above me the day-blind stars
waiting with their light. For a time
I rest in the grace of the world, and am free.

WENDELL BERRY, B. 1934

PLASH MILL, UNDER THE MOOR

The wind leapt, mad-wolf, over the rim of the moor
At a single bound, and with furious uproar
Fell on the tree-ringed house by the deep-cut stream —
Quiet little house standing alone,
Blind, old, pale as the moon,
And sunk in some ancient grassy dream.

Through all the roaring maniac din
Outside, the shadowless stillness there within
Held. No face, all the frantic day,
Pressed the glass, watching the green apple hailstorm,
No child's heart gladdened at thought of where acorns lay,
And beechnuts, treasure for harvesting safe from harm.

... But when, next March perhaps, sunlight the colour of frost
Wavers through branches to honeycomb some flaking wall
Changeless since autumn that will be the utmost
Hope realised: light's delicate miracle
Of grace
Still wrought on the forsaken place.

FRANCES BELLERBY

TO HAFIZ OF SHIRAZ

The rose has come into the garden, from
        Nothingness into being.

Once I did not know the birds were described,
classified, observed, fixed in their proper localities.
Each bird that sprang from the tree, passed overhead,
  hawked from the bough,
was sole, new, dressed as no other was dressed.
Any leaf might hide the paradise-bird.

Once I believed any poem might follow my pen,
any road might beckon my feet to mapless horizons,
any eyes that I met, any hand that I took, any word that
  I heard,
might pierce to my heart, stay forever in mine, open worlds
  on its hinge.
All then seemed possible; time and world were my own.

Now that I know that each star has its path, each bird
is finally feathered and grown in the unbroken shell,
each tree in the seed, each song in the life laid down —
is the night sky any less strange; should my glance less follow
  the flight;
should the pen shake less in my hand?

No, more and more like a birth looks the scheduled rising of Venus:
the turn of a wing in the wind more startles my blood.
Every path and life leads one way only,
out of continual miracle, through creation's fable,
over and over repeated but never yet understood....

JUDITH WRIGHT. B. 1915

Some nights, stay up till dawn...
Be a full bucket pulled up the dark way
of a well, then lifted out into light.

Something opens our wings. Something
makes boredom and hurt disappear.
Something fills the cup in front of us.
We taste only sacredness.

JALAL AD-DIN AR-RUMI,

(c.1207-1273)

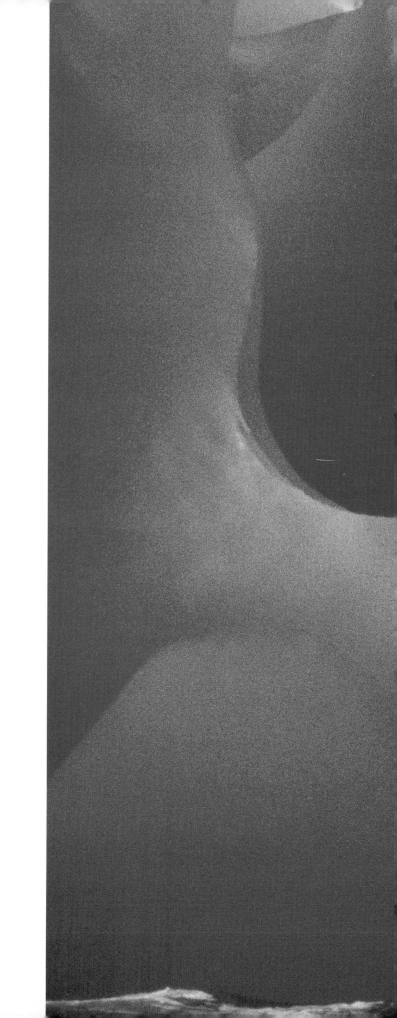

O warmth of summer

gliding over the land in waves!

Not a gust of wind,

not a cloud —

And in the mountains,

the belling reindeer,

the sweet reindeer

in the bluish distance!

O, how it pulls me,

O, how it fills me with delight!

Sobbing with emotion,

I lie down on the earth.

AUTHOR UNKNOWN (ESKIMO)

At the furthest wavelength of thought, the sea and the wind and the trees and sand are... me. It is a thought that blinks into the mind, like a giant laughing eye, and then is gone for a long, long time.

ROBERT HUNTER (1874-1942)

FROM UNDERNEATH

*A giant sea turtle saved the life of a 52 year old woman
lost at sea for two days after a shipwreck in the Southern Philippines.
She rode on the turtle's back.*

SYRACUSE POST-STANDARD

When her arms were no longer
strong enough to tread water
it came up beneath her, hard
and immense, and she thought
this is how death comes,
something large between your legs
and then the plunge.
She dived off instinctively,
but it got beneath her again
and when she realized what it was
she soiled herself, held on.

God would have sent something winged,
she thought. *This* came from beneath,
a piece of hell that killed a turtle
on the way and took its shape.
How many hours passed?
She didn't know, but it was night
and the waves were higher.
The thing swam easily in the dark.

She swooned into sleep.
When she woke it was morning,
the sea calm, her strange raft
still moving. She noticed the elaborate
pattern of its shell, map-like,
the leathery neck and head
as if she'd come up behind
an old longshoreman
in a hard-backed chair.

She wanted and was afraid to touch
the head – one finger
just above the eyes –
the way she could touch her cat
and make it hers.
The more it swam a steady course
the more she spoke to it
the jibberish of the lost.
And then the laughter
located at the bottom
of oneself, unstoppable.

The call went from sailor to sailor
on the fishing boat: A woman
riding an "oil drum"
off the starboard side.
But the turtle was already swimming
toward the prow
with its hysterical, foreign cargo
and when it came up alongside
it stopped
until she could be hoisted off.
Then it circled three times
and went down.
The woman was beyond all language,
the captain reported;
the crew was afraid of her
for a long, long time.

STEPHEN DUNN

WHALES WEEP NOT!

They say the sea is cold, but the sea contains
the hottest blood of all, and the wildest, the most urgent.

All the whales in the wider deeps, hot are they, as they urge
on and on, and dive beneath the icebergs.
The right whales, the sperm-whales, the hammer-heads,
    the killers
there they blow, there they blow, hot wild white breath
    out of the sea!

And they rock, and they rock, through the sensual ageless ages
on the depths of the seven seas,
and through the salt they reel with drunk delight
and in the tropics tremble they with love
and roll with massive, strong desire, like gods.
Then the great bull lies up against his bride
in the blue deep bed of sea,
as mountain pressing on mountain, in the zest of life:
and out of the inward roaring of the inner red ocean of
    whale-blood
the long tip reaches strong, intense, like the maelstrom-tip,
    and comes to rest
in the clasp and the soft, wild clutch of a she-whale's
    fathomless body.

And over the bridge of the whale's strong phallus, linking the
    wonder of whales
the burning archangels under the sea keep passing, back and forth,
keep passing, archangels of bliss
from him to her, from her to him great Cherubim
that wait on whales in mid-ocean, suspended in the waves of
    the sea.
great heaven of whales in the waters, old hierarchies.

And enormous mother whales lie dreaming suckling their
    whale-tender young
and dreaming with strange whale eyes wide open in the waters
    of the beginning and the end.

And bull-whales gather their women and whale-calves in a ring
when danger threatens, on the surface of the ceaseless flood
and range themselves like great fierce Seraphim facing the threat
encircling their huddled monsters of love.

And all this happens in the sea, in the salt
where God is also love, but without words:
And Aphrodite is the wife of whales
most happy, happy she!

and Venus among the fishes skips and is a she-dolphin
she is the gay, delighted porpoise sporting with love and the sea
she is female tunny-fish, round and happy among the males
and dense with happy blood, dark rainbow bliss in the sea.

D.H. LAWRENCE (1885-1930)

AFTER I CAME BACK FROM ICELAND

After I came back from Iceland,
I couldn't stop talking. It was the light,
you see, the light and the air. I tried to put it
into poems, even, but you couldn't write

the waterfall on White River, blinding
and glacial, nor the clean toy town
with the resplendent harbour for its glass.
you couldn't write how the black lava shone,

nor how the outlines of the bright red roofs
cut the sky sharp as a knife; how breathing
was like drinking cold water. When I got back
to Heathrow and walked out into Reading,

I damn near choked on this warm gritty stuff
I called air: also on the conjecture
that we'd all settle for second best
once we'd forgotten there was something more.

SHEENAGH PUGH

DELIGHT IN NATURE

Isn't it delightful,
little river cutting through the gorge,
when you slowly approach it,
and trout hang behind stones
in the stream?
   Jajai-ija.

Isn't it delightful,
that grassy river bank?
Yet Willow Twig.
whom I so long to see again,
is lost to me.
So be it.
The winding of the river
through the gorge is lovely enough
   Jajai-ija.

Isn't it delightful
that bluish island of rocks out there,
as you slowly approach it?
So what does it matter
that the blowing spirit of the air
wanders over the rocks:
the island is so beautiful....

AUTHOR UNKNOWN (ESKIMO)

The great sea
Has sent me adrift.
It moves me
as the weed
in a great river.
Earth and the great weather
move me,
have carried me away,
and move my inward parts
with joy.

UVAVNUK, ESKIMO SHAMAN WOMAN

The shore is an ancient world, for as long as there has been an earth and sea there has been this place of the meeting of land and water. Yet it is a world that keeps alive the sense of continuing creation and of the relentless drive of life. Each time that I enter it, I gain some new awareness of its beauty and its deeper meanings, sensing that intricate fabric of life by which one creature is linked with another, and each with its surroundings....

There is a common thread that links these scenes and memories – the spectacle of life in all its varied manifestations as it has appeared, evolved, and sometimes died out. Underlying the beauty of the spectacle there is meaning and significance. It is the elusiveness of that meaning that haunts us, that sends us again and again into the natural world where the key to the riddle is hidden. It sends us back to the edge of the sea, where the drama of life played its first scene on earth and perhaps even its prelude; where the forces of evolution are at work today, as they have been since the appearance of what we know as life; and where the spectacle of living creatures faced by the cosmic realities of their world is crystal clear.

RACHEL CARSON (1907-1964)

JUNE 20, 1853

Found two lilies open in the very shallow inlet of the meadow.
Exquisitely beautiful, and unlike anything else we have, is the first white lily
just expanded in some shallow lagoon where the water is leaving it, – perfectly
fresh and pure, before the insects have discovered it.
How admirable its purity! How innocentely sweet its fragrance! How
significant that the rich, black mud of our dead stream produces the water-lily,
– out of that fertile slime springs this spotless purity! It is remarkable that
those flowers which are most emblematical of purity should grow in the mud.

HENRY DAVID THOREAU (1817-1862)

THE VERY LEAVES OF THE ACACIA-TREE ARE LONDON

The very leaves of the acacia-tree are London;
London tap-water fills out the fuchsia buds in the back garden,
Blackbirds pull London worms out of the sour soil,
The woodlice, centipedes, eat London, the wasps even.
London air through stomata of myriad leaves
And million lungs of London breathes.
Chlorophyll and haemoglobin do what life can
To purify, to return this great explosion
To sanity of leaf and wing.
Gradual and gentle the growth of London Pride,
And sparrows are free of all the time in the world:
Less than a window-pane between.

KATHLEEN RAINE, B.1908

COME HITHER

Come hither, ye who thirst;
Pure still the brook flows on;
Its waters are not curst;
Clear from its rock of stone
It bubbles and it boils,
An evelasting rill,
Then eddies and recoils
And wimples clearer still.
Art troubled? then come hither,
And taste of peace for ever.

Art weary? here's the place
For weariness to rest,
These flowers are herbs of grace
To cure the aching breast;
Soft beds these mossy banks
Where dewdrops only weep,
Where Nature 'turns God thanks
And sings herself to sleep.
Art troubled with strife? come hither,
Here's peace and summer weather.

Come hither for pleasure who list —
Here are oak boughs for a shade:
These leaves they will hide from the mist
Ere the sun his broad disk has displayed.
Here is peace if thy bosom be troubled,
Here is rest — if thou'rt weary, sit down
Here pleasure you'll find it is doubled,
For content is life's only crown.
Disciples of sorrow, come hither,
For no blasts my joys can wither.

... The world is all lost in commotion,
The blind lead the blind into strife;
Come hither, thou wreck of life's ocean,
Let solitude warm thee to life.
Be the pilgrim of love and the joy of its sorrow,
Be anything but the world's man:
The dark of to-day brings the sun of to-morrow,
Be proud that your joy here began.
Poor shipwreck of life, journey hither,
And we'll talk of life's troubles together.

JOHN CLARE (1793-1864)

What would the world be, once bereft
Of wet and wildness? Let them be left
O let them be left, wildness and wet;
Long live the weeds and the wilderness yet.

GERARD MANLEY HOPKINS (1844-1889), FROM "INVERSNAID"

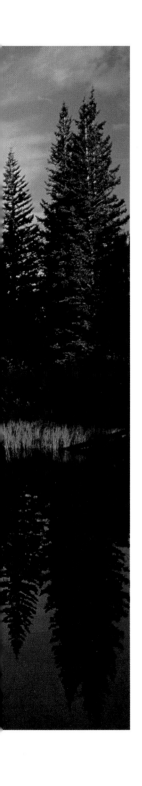

O if we but knew what we do
When we delve or hew –
Hack and rack the growing green!
Where we, even where we mean
To mend we end her,
When we hew or delve:
After-comers cannot guess the beauty been.

GERARD MANLEY HOPKINS (1844-1889),
FROM "BINSEY POPLARS"

Those who would take over the earth

And shape it to their will

Never, I notice, succeed.

The earth is like a vessel so sacred

That at the mere approach of the profane

It is marred

And when they reach out their fingers it is gone.

For a time the world some force themselves ahead

And some are left behind,

For a time in the world some make a great noise

And some are held silent,

For a time in the world some are puffed fat

And some are kept hungry,

For a time in the world some push aboard

And some are tipped out;

At no time in the world will a man who is sane

Over-reach himself,

Over-spend himself,

Over-rate himself.

LAO TZU (c.604-531B.C.)

Most people want to preserve the forest as a "resource", so that they can take whatever they feel it has to give. This is a very dangerous act – you are taking nature hostage.

You finally subdue her so that you can take what you want: if she does not give you what you want you cut more forest, dig more deeply, throw on more agricultural toxins, disfiguring her body and disregarding her rhythms.

All knowledge of our people is based on a permanent relationship with the places we live. We live with a magical perspective. The people who live in a valley see rivers and mountains in a very different way from a geologist or a biologist. A mountain for us has a name... has a history, a story to tell.

When we go into the forest we discover our relationship with life. The blood of the forest is the sap, it runs through the tree until it meets the leaves.

People need to see that they live in a wonderful world.

People must not lose their hope.

In the forest, do you think that it is possible to organise thousands of workers, to make them get up and go to work every day, then come back, sleep, get up, work, sleep, work? It is impossible – the forest conspires with human beings to create pleasures.

We have lived in this place for a long time, a very long time.... We learned with the ancients that we are a tiny part of this immense universe, fellow travellers with all the animals, the plants and the waters.

We are all part of the whole, we cannot neglect or destroy our home.

And now we want to talk to those who cannot yet manage to see the world in this way, to say to them that together we have to take care of the boat in which we are all sailing.

If the human beings who are encouraging the existence of this kind of civilisation are able to anticipate what is going to happen – why do they continue?

If we continue to treat our planet as a suburb, dividing her into many plots and quarters, we will eventually destroy the fabric of life.

We can either keep trying to control the events of the world or understand that we are just an event in the life of the world.

AILTON KRENAK (NATIONAL CO-ORDINATOR OF THE UNION OF INDIAN NATIONS AND PRESIDENT OF THE FOREST PEOPLE'S ALLIANCE,

WHICH REPRESENTS THOUSANDS OF AMAZONIAN INDIANS.)

... Myself was lost,

Gone from me like an ache, and what remained

Became a part of the universal joy.

My soul went forth, and mingling with the tree,

Danced in the leaves; or floating in the cloud,

Saw its white double in the stream below;

Or else sublimed to purer ecstasy,

Dilated in the broad blue over all.

I was the wind that dappled the lush grass,

The thin-winged swallow skating on the air;

The life that gladdened everything was mine.

JAMES RUSSELL LOWELL (1819-1891)

THE SPHERE

Oh the happy ending, the happy ending
That the fugue promised, that love believed in,
That perfect star, that bright transfiguration,

Where has it vanished, now that the music is over,
The certainty of being, the heart in flower,
Ourselves, perfect at last, affirmed as what we are?

The world, the changing world stands still while lovers kiss,
And then moves on – what was our fugitive bliss,
The dancer's ecstasy, the vision, and the rose?

There is no end, no ending – steps of a dance, petals of flowers
Phrases of music, rays of the sun, the hours
Succeed each other, and the perfect sphere
Turns in our hearts the past and future, near and far,
Our single soul, atom, and universe.

KATHLEEN RAINE, B. 1908

Viewed from the distance of the moon, the astonishing thing about the earth, catching the breath, is that it is alive. The photographs show the dry, pounded surface of the moon in the foreground, dead as an old bone. Aloft, floating free beneath the moist, gleaming membrane of bright blue sky, is the rising earth, the only exuberant thing in this part of the cosmos. If you could look long enough, you would see the swirling of the great drifts of white cloud, covering and uncovering the half-hidden masses of land. If you had been looking for a very long, geologic time, you could have seen the continents themselves in motion, drifting apart on their crustal plates, held aloft by the fire beneath. It has the organized, self-contained look of a live creature, full of information, marvellously skilled in handling the sun.

LEWIS THOMAS, FROM "THE LIVES OF A CELL"

If the Earth were only a few feet in diameter, floating a few feet above a field somewhere, people would come from everywhere to marvel at it.... The people would marvel at all the creatures walking around the surface of the ball and at the creatures in the water. The people would declare it as sacred because it was the only one, and they would protect it so that it would not be hurt. The ball would be the greatest wonder known, and people would come to pray to it, to be healed, to gain knowledge, to know beauty and to wonder how it could be.

JOE MILLER

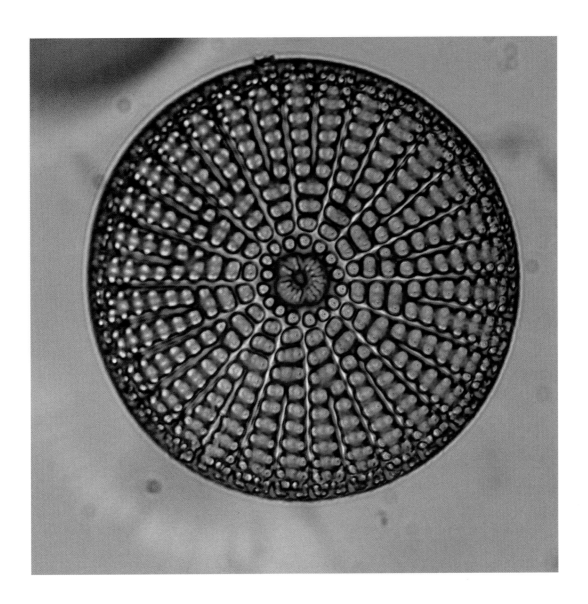

No matter how deeply we look into the fabric of material being —
the biological level, chemical level, subatomic level — we see that life
forms are interdependent, co-conditioning and co-evolving. Every
human effort, civilisation, thought, and spiritual insight, requires
and is supported by the whole of organic life.

RICK FIELDS

WINTER MEMORIES

Within the circuit of this plodding life

There enter moments of an azure hue,

Untarnished fair as is the violet

Or anemone, when the spring strews them

By some meandering rivulet, which make

The best philosophy untrue that aims

But to console man for his grievances.

... When all the fields around lay bound and hoar

Beneath a thick integument of snow.

So by God's cheap economy made rich

To go upon my winter's task again.

HENRY DAVID THOREAU (1817-1862)

Up in this high air, you breathed easily, drawing in a vital assurance and lightness of heart. In the highlands, you woke up in the morning and thought: "Here I am, where I ought to be."

ISAK DINESEN (1885 - 1962)

I awoke in the early morning when the train stopped with a long sibilant sigh at the Italian frontier. The sunlight was seeping round the edges of the drawn blind, illuminating the dust particles which filled the air, and I leaned across my bunk and pulled it aside.

For the first time I saw snow-covered mountains against a clear blue sky. I was completely overwhelmed by their unearthly beauty. It was like a vision or a religious revelation, and remained with me all my life.

I let down the window and leaned out, discovering that mountain air involves a special experience of clarity and timelessness. Since then I have spent thirty winters at high altitude in the Alps. From my window, I could watch the first rays of the rising sun gild the saddle between two snow-covered peaks or the shadows in the glacier turn green when a warm wind threatened. High up the valley before it grew light you could hear the chimes of the snowfinches' dawn chorus. I tinker with Byron's poem:

> Art, Glory, Freedom fail,
> But Mountains still are fair.

During the Second World War I did not sigh for petrol coupons or chocolate or sugar or a new dress – what I dreamed of was mountain air and the way sound travels across the valley.

MIRIAM ROTHSCHILD (ZOOLOGIST)

IN MIDWINTER A WOOD WAS

In midwinter a wood was
where the sand-coloured deer ran
through quietness.
It was a marvellous thing
to see those deer running.

Softer than ashes
snow lay all winter where they ran,
and in the wood a holly tree was.
God, it was a marvellous thing
to see the deer running.

Between lime trunks grey or green
branch-headed stags went by
silently trotting.
A holly tree dark and crimson
sprouted at the wood's centre, thick and high
without a whisper, no other berry so fine.

Outside the wood was black midwinter,
over the downs that reared so solemn
wind rushed in gales, and strong here
wrapped around wood and holly fire
(where deer among the close limes ran)
with a storming circle of its thunder.
Under the trees it was a marvellous thing
to see the deer running.

PETER LEVI

MAPLE AND SUMACH

Maple and sumach down this autumn ride —
Look, in what scarlet character they speak!
For this their russet and rejoicing week
Trees spend a year of sunsets on their pride.
You leaves drenched with the lifeblood of the year —
What flamingo dawns have wavered from the east,
What eves have crimsoned to their toppling crest
To give the fame and transience that you wear!
Leaf-low he shall lie soon: but no such blaze
Briefly can cheer man's ashen, harsh decline;
His fall is short of pride, he bleeds within
And paler creeps to the dead end of his days.
O light's abandon and the fire-crest sky
Speak in me now for all who are to die

C. DAY LEWIS (1904-1972)

An owl sat once with his sharp hearing, his watchfulness,
his bill, half-grown, majestic on my finger;
then I felt his huge and yellow stare
plant something foreign in me, a deep quiet,
a mad freedom; my heart laughed
when the bird raised his soft wings.

THORKILD BJORNVIG, B.1918, FROM "THE OWL"

Wind is thin,
sun warm,
the earth overflows
with good things.

Spring is purple
jewelry;
flowers on the ground,
green in the forest.

Quadrupeds shine
and wander. Birds
nest. On blossoming
branches they cry joy!

My eyes see, my ears
hear so much, and
I am thrilled.
Yet I swallow sighs.

Sitting here alone,
I turn pale. When strong
enough to lift my head,
I hear and see nothing.

Spring, hear me.
Despite green woods,
blossoms and seed,
my spirit rots.

AUTHOR UNKNOWN
(MEDIEVAL LATIN, C. 1000 A.D.
FROM "THE CAMBRIDGE SONGS")

IF BIRTH PERSISTS

He sees the gentle stir of birth
When morning purifies the earth;
He leans upon a gate and sees
The pastures, and the quiet trees.
Low, woody hill, with gracious bound,
Folds the still valley almost round;
The cuckoo, loud on some high lawn,
Is answered from the depth of dawn;
In the hedge straggling to the stream,
Pale, dew-drenched, half-shut roses gleam;
But, where the farther side slopes down,
He sees the drowsy new-waked clown
In his white quaint-embroidered frock
Make, whistling, tow'rd his mist-wreathed flock –
Slowly, behind his heavy tread,
The wet, flowered grass heaves up its head.
Leaned on his gate, he gazes – tears
Are in his eyes, and in his ears
The murmur of a thousand years.
Before him he sees life unroll,
A placid and continuous whole –
That general life, which does not cease,
Whose secret is not joy, but peace;
That life, whose dumb wish is not missed
If birth proceeds, if things subsist;
The life of plants, and stones, and rain,
The life he craves – if not in vain
Fate gave, what chance shall not control,
His sad lucidity of soul.

MATTHEW ARNOLD (1822-1888)

MAY 23, 1854

We soon get through with Nature. She excites an expectation which she cannot satisfy. The merest child which has rambled into a copsewood dreams of a wildness so wild and strange and inexhaustible as Nature can never show him.... There was a time when the beauty and the music were all within, and I sat and listened to my thoughts, and there was a song in them. I sat for hours on rocks and wrestled with the melody which possessed me. I sat and listened by the hour to a positive though faint and distant music, not sung by any bird, nor vibrating any earthly harp. When you walked with a joy which knew not its own origin. When you were an organ of which the world was but one poor broken pipe. I lay long on the rocks, foundered like a harp on the seashore, that knows not how it is dealt with. You sat on the earth as on a raft, listening to music that was not of the earth, but which ruled and arranged it. Man *should be* the harp articulate. When you cords were tense.

HENRY DAVID THOREAU (1817-1862)

AUTUMN ON THE LAND

A man, a field, silence — what is there to say?
He lives, he moves, and the October day
Burns slowly down
              History is made
Elsewhere; the hours forfeit to time's blade
Don't matter here. The leaves large and small,
Shed by the branches, unlamented fall
About his shoulders. You may look in vain
Through the eyes' window; on his meagre hearth
The thin, shy soul has not begun its reign
Over the darkness. Beauty, love and mirth
And joy are strangers there.
                  You must revise
Your bland philosophy of nature, earth
Has of itself no power to make men wise.

R.S. THOMAS, B.1913

TINTERN ABBEY

Written a few miles above Tintern Abbey,
on revisiting the banks of the Wye during a tour.
July 13, 1798

Five years have passed; five summers, with the length
Of five long winters! and again I hear
These waters, rolling from their mountain-springs
With a soft inland murmur. – Once again
Do I behold these steep and lofty cliffs,
That on a wild secluded scene impress
Thoughts of more deep seclusion; and connect
The landscape with the quiet of the sky.
The day is come when I again repose
Here, under this dark sycamore, and view
These plots of cottage-ground, these orchard-tufts,
Which at this season, with their unripe fruits,
Are clad in one green hue, and lose themselves
'Mid groves and copses. Once again I see
These hedge-rows, hardly hedge-rows, little lines
Of sportive wood run wild: these pastoral farms
Green to the very door; and wreaths of smoke
Sent up, in silence, from among the trees!
With some uncertain notice, as might seem,
Of vagrant dwellers in the houseless woods,
Or of some Hermit's cave, where by his fire
The Hermit sits alone.
                              These beauteous forms,
Through a long absence, have not been to me,
As is a landscape to a blind man's eye:
But oft, in lonely rooms, and 'mid the din
Of towns and cities, I have owed to them,
In hours of weariness, sensations sweet,
Felt in the blood, and felt along the heart;
And passing even into my purer mind,
With tranquil restoration: – feelings too
Of unremembered pleasure: such, perhaps,
As have no slight or trivial influence
On that best portion of a good man's life,
His little, nameless, unremembered acts
Of kindness and of love. Nor less, I trust,
To them I may have owed another gift,

Of aspect more sublime; that blessed mood,
In which the burthen of the mystery,
In which the heavy and the weary weight
Of all this unintelligible world,
Is lightened: — that serene and blessed mood,
In which the affections gently lead us on, —
Until, the breath of this corporeal frame,
And even the motion of our human blood
Almost suspended, we are laid asleep
In body, and become a living soul:
While with an eye made quiet by the power
Of harmony, and the deep power of joy,
We see into the life of things.
                                   If this
Be but a vain belief, yet, oh! how oft —
In darkness and amid the many shapes
Of joyless daylight; when the fretful stir
Unprofitable, and the fever of the world,
Have hung upon the beatings of my heart —
How oft, in spirit, have I turned to thee,
O sylvan Wye! thou wanderer thro' the woods,
How often has my spirit turned to thee!

And now, with gleams of half-extinguished thought,
With many recognitions dim and faint,
And somewhat of a sad perplexity,
The picture of the mind revives again:
While here I stand, not only with the sense
Of present pleasure, but with pleasing thoughts
That in this moment there is life and food
For future years. And so I dare to hope,
Though changed, no doubt, from what I was when first
I came among these hills; when like a roe
I bounded o'er the mountains, by the sides
Of the deep rivers, and the lonely streams,
Wherever nature led: more like a man
Flying from something that he dreads than one
Who sought the thing he loved. For nature then
(The coarser pleasures of my boyish days,
And their glad animal movements all gone by)
To me was all in all. — I cannot paint
What then I was. The sounding cataract

Haunted me like a passion: the tall rock,
The mountain, and the deep and gloomy wood,
Their colours and their forms, were then to me
An appetite; a feeling and a love,
That had no need of a remoter charm,
By thought supplied, nor any interest
Unborrowed from the eye. – That time is past,
And all its aching joys are now no more,
And all its dizzy raptures. Not for this
Faint I, nor mourn nor murmur: other gifts
Have followed; for such loss, I would believe,
Abundant recompense. For I have learned
To look on nature, not as in the hour
Of thoughtless youth; but hearing oftentimes
The still, sad music of humanity,
Nor harsh nor grating, though of ample power
To chasten and subdue. And I have felt
A presence that disturbs me with the joy
Of elevated thoughts; a sense sublime
Of something far more deeply interfused,
Whose dwelling is the light of setting suns,
And the round ocean and the living air,
And the blue sky, and in the mind of man:
A motion and a spirit, that impels
All thinking things, all objects of all thought,
And rolls through all things. Therefore am I still
A lover of the meadows and the woods,
And mountains; and of all that we behold
From this green earth; of all the mighty world
Of eye, and ear, – both what they half create,
And what perceive; well pleased to recognise
In nature and the language of the sense
The anchor of my purest thoughts, the nurse,
The guide, the guardian of my heart, and soul
Of all my moral being....

WILLIAM WORDSWORTH (1770-1850)

MESSAGE FROM HOME

Do you remember, when you were first a child,
Nothing in the world seemed strange to you?
You perceived, for the first time, shapes already familiar,
And seeing, you knew that you had always known
The lichen on the rock, fern-leaves, the flowers of thyme,
As if the elements newly met in your body,
Caught up into the momentary vortex of your living
Still kept the knowledge of a former state,
In you retained recollection of cloud and ocean,
The branching tree, the dancing flame.

Now when nature's darkness seems strange to you,
And you walk, an alien, in the streets of cities,
Remember earth breathed you into her with the air,
     with the sun's rays,
Laid you in her waters asleep, to dream
With the brown trout among the milfoil roots,
From substance of star and ocean fashioned you,
At the same source conceived you
As sun and foliage, fish and stream.

Of all created things the source is one,
Simple, single as love; remember
The cell and seed of life, the sphere
That is, of child, white bird, and small blue dragon-fly
Green fern, and the gold four-petalled tormentilla
The ultimate memory.
Each latent cell puts out a future,
Unfolds its differing complexity
As a tree puts forth leaves, and spins a fate
Fern-traced, bird-feathered, or fish-scaled.

Moss spreads its green film on the moist peat,
The germ of dragon-fly pulses into animation and
    takes wing
As the water-lily from the mud ascends on its ropy stem
To open a sweet white calyx to the sky.
Man, with farther to travel from his simplicity,
From the archaic moss, fish, and lily parts,
And into exile travels his long way.

... Nothing in that abyss is alien to you.
Sleep at the tree's root, where the night is spun
Into the stuff of worlds, listen to the winds,
The tides, and the night's harmonies, and know
All that you knew before you began to forget,
Before you became estranged from your own being,
Before you had too long parted from those other
More simple children, who have stayed at home
In meadow and island and forest, in sea and river.
Earth sends a mother's love after her exiled son....

KATHLEEN RAINE, B.1908

... yellow running jasmin vine,
cape jessamine and saucer magnolias:
tulip-shaped, scenting lemon musk upon the air.
My Mississippi Spring —
my warm loving heart a-fire
with early greening leaves,
dogwoood branches laced against the sky;
wild forest nature paths
heralding Resurrection over and over again
... every Mississippi Spring!

MARGARET WALKER, FROM "MY MISSISSIPPI SPRING"

SPRING

Nothing is so beautiful as Spring —
When weeds, in wheels, shoot long and lovely and lush:
What is all this juice and all this joy?

GERARD MANLEY HOPKINS (1844-1889)

COME INTO ANIMAL PRESENCE

... What is this joy? That no animal
falters, but knows what it must do?
That the snake has no blemish,
that the rabbit inspects his strange surroundings
in white star-silence? The llama
rests in dignity, the armadillo
has some intention to pursue in the palm-forest.
Those who were sacred have remained so,
holiness does not dissolve, it is a presence
of bronze, only the sight that saw it
faltered and turned from it.
An old joy returns in holy presence.

DENISE LEVERTOV

SOME QUESTIONS YOU MIGHT ASK

Is the soul solid, like iron?
Or is it tender and breakable, like
the wings of a moth in the beak of an owl?
Who has it, and who doesn't?
I keep looking around me.
The face of a moose is as sad
as the face of Jesus.
The swan opens her white wings slowly.
In the fall, the black bear carries leaves into the darkness.
One question leads to another.
Does it have a shape? Like an iceberg?
Like the eye of a hummingbird?
Does it have one lung, like the snake and the scallop?
Why should I have it, and not the anteater
who loves her children?
Why should I have it, and not the camel?
Come to think of it, what about the maple trees?
What about the blue iris?
What about all the little stones, sitting alone in the moonlight?
What about roses, and lemons, and their shining leaves?
What about the grass?

MARY OLIVER, B. 1935

THE DALLIANCE OF THE EAGLES

Skirting the river road, (my forenoon walk, my rest,)
Skyward in air a sudden muffled sound, the dalliance of the eagles,
The rushing amorous contact high in space together,
The clinching interlocking claws, a living, fierce, gyrating wheel,
Four beating wings, two beaks, a swirling mass tight grappling,
In tumbling turning clustering loops, straight downward falling,
Till o'er the river pois'd, the twain yet one, a moment's lull,
A motionless still balance in the air, then parting, talons loosing,
Upward again on slow-firm pinions slanting, their separate
  diverse flight,
She hers, he his, pursuing.

WALT WHITMAN (1819-1892)

PROUD SONGSTERS

These are brand-new birds of twelve-months' growing,
Which a year ago, or less than twain,
No finches were, nor nightingales,
Nor thrushes,
But only particles of grain,
And earth and air, and rain.

THOMAS HARDY (1840-1928)

BATS

A bat is born
Naked and blind and pale.
His mother makes a pocket of her tail
And catches him. He clings to her long fur
By his thumbs and toes and teeth.
And then the mother dances through the night
Doubling and looping, soaring, somersaulting –
Her baby hangs on underneath.
All night, in happiness, she hunts and flies.
Her high sharp cries
Like shining needlepoints of sound
Go out into the night, and echoing back,
Tell her what they have touched.
She hears how far it is, how big it is,
Which way it's going:
She lives by hearing.
The mother eats the moths and gnats she catches
In full flight; in full flight
The mother drinks the water of the pond
She skims across. Her baby hangs on tight.
Her baby drinks the milk she makes him
In moonlight or starlight, in mid-air.
Their single shadow, printed on the moon
Or fluttering across the stars,
Whirls on all night; at daybreak
The tired mother flaps home to her rafter.
The others all are there.
They hang themselves up by their toes,
They wrap themselves in their brown wings.
Bunched upside-down, they sleep in air.
Their sharp ears, their sharp teeth, their quick sharp faces
Are dull and slow and mild.
All the bright day, as the mother sleeps,
She folds her wings about her sleeping child.

RANDALL JARRELL

From THE WATERBUCK

He has not stood there all these years just waiting
To perform on memory's loop, or trusting
That a poem would occur: now for the first time
I see the accusing simplicity of his claim
For continuance, for nothing more than simple justice.

LAWRENCE SAIL

... POWERFUL GRACE THAT LIES

IN HERBS, PLANTS, STONES, AND THEIR QUALITIES:

FOR NAUGHT SO VILE THAT ON THE EARTH DOTH LIVE

BUT TO THE EARTH SOME SPECIAL FOOD DOTH GIVE.

WILLIAM SHAKESPEARE (1564-1616)

WOOD RIDES

Who hath not felt the influence that so calms

The weary mind in summers sultry hours

When wandering thickest woods beneath the arms

Of ancient oaks and brushing nameless flowers

That verge the little ride who hath not made

A minutes waste of time and sat him down

Upon a pleasant swell to gaze awhile

On crowding ferns bluebells and hazel leaves

... Who hath (not) met that mood from turmoil free

And felt a placid joy refreshed at heart

J O H N   C L A R E   (1 7 9 3 - 1 8 6 4)

NUTTING

It seems a day
(I speak of one from many singled out)
One of those heavenly days that cannot die;
When, in the eagerness of boyish hope,
I left our cottage-threshold, sallying forth
With a huge wallet o'er my shoulders slung,
A nutting-crook in hand; and turned my steps
Tow'rd some far-distant wood...

                ... O'er pathless rocks,
Through beds of matted fern, and tangled thickets,
Forcing my way, I came to one dear nook
Unvisited, where not a broken bough
Drooped with its withered leaves, ungracious sign
Of devastation; but the hazels rose
Tall and erect, with tempting clusters hung,
A virgin scene! — A little while I stood,
Breathing with such suppression of the heart
As joy delights in; and with wise restraint
Voluptuous, fearless of a rival, eyed
The banquet; — or beneath the trees I sate
Among the flowers, and with the flowers I played;
... Perhaps it was a bower beneath whose leaves
The violets of five seasons re-appear
And fade, unseen by any human eye;
Where fairy water-breaks do murmur on
For ever; and I saw the sparkling foam,
And — with my cheek on one of those green stones
That, fleeced with moss, under the shady trees,
Lay round me, scattered like a flock of sheep —
I heard the murmur and the murmuring sound,
In that sweet mood when pleasure loves to pay
Tribute to ease; and, of its joy secure,
The heart luxuriates with indifferent things,
Wasting its kindliness on stocks and stones,
And on the vacant air. Then up I rose,
And dragged to earth both branch and bough, with crash
And merciless ravage: and the shady nook
Of hazels, and the green and mossy bower,

Deformed and sullied, patiently gave up
Their quiet being: and unless I now
Confound my present feelings with the past,
Ere from the mutilated bower I turned
Exulting, rich beyond the wealth of kings,
I felt a sense of pain when I beheld
The silent trees, and saw the intruding sky. –
Then, dearest Maiden, move along these shades
In gentleness of heart; with gentle hand
Touch – for there is a spirit in the woods.

WILLIAM WORDSWORTH (1770-1850)

ENCLOSURE

Far spread the moory ground, a level scene
Bespread with rush and one eternal green,
That never felt the rage of blundering plough,
Though centuries wreathed spring blossoms on its brow.
Autumn met plains that stretched them far away
In unchecked shadows of green, brown, and grey.
Unbounded freedom ruled the wandering scene;
No fence of ownership crept in between
To hide the prospect from the gazing eye;
Its only bondage was the circling sky.
A mighty flat, undwarfed by bush and tree,
Spread its faint shadow of immensity,
And lost itself, which seemed to eke its bounds,
In the blue mist the horizon's edge surrounds.
Now this sweet vision of my boyish hours,
Free as spring clouds and wild as forest flowers,
Is faded all – a hope that blossomed free,
And hath been once as it no more shall be.
Enclosure came, and trampled on the grave
Of labour's rights, and left the poor a slave;
And memory's pride, ere want to wealth did bow,
Is both the shadow and the substance now.
... But now all's fled and flats of many a dye
That seemed to lengthen with the following eye,
... Are banished now with heaths once wild and gay
As poet's visions of life's early day.
Like mighty giants of their limbs bereft,
The skybound wastes in mangled garbs are left,
Fence meeting fence in owner's little bounds
Of field and meadow, large as garden-grounds,
In little parcels little minds to please,
With men and flocks imprisoned, ill at ease.
For with the poor scared freedom bade farewell,
And fortune-hunters totter where they fell;
They dreamed of riches in the rebel scheme
And find too truly that they did but dream.

JOHN CLARE (1793-1864)

Now, my co-mates and brothers in exile,

Hath not old customs made this life more sweet

Than that of painted pomp? Are not these woods

More free from peril than the envious court!

Here feel we not the penalty of Adam,

The seasons' difference; as the icy fang

And churlish chiding of the winter's wind,

Which when it bites and blows upon my body,

Even till I shrink with cold, I smile and say

"This is no flattery; these are counsellors

That feelingly persuade me what I am".

Sweet are the uses of adversity;

Which, like the toad, ugly and venomous,

Wears yet a precious jewel in his head;

And this our life, exempt from public haunt,

Finds tongues in trees, books in the running brooks,

Sermons in stones, and good in everything.

I would not change it.

WILLIAM SHAKESPEARE (1564-1616),
FROM "AS YOU LIKE IT"

... this curious world which we inhabit is more wonderful than it is convenient; more beautiful than it is useful; it is more to be admired and enjoyed than used.

HENRY DAVID THOREAU (1817-1862)

WE PAUSED AMID THE PINES
THAT STOOD...

… How calm it was – the silence there
    By such a chain was bound,
That even the busy woodpecker
    Made stiller by her sound

The inviolable quietness;
    The breath of peace we drew
With its soft motion made not less
    The calm that round us grew.

It seemed that from the remotest seat
    Of the white mountain's waste
To the bright flower beneath our feet,
    A magic circle traced; –

A spirit interfused around,
    A thinking, silent life;
To momentary peace it bound
Our mortal nature's strife; –

And still, it seemed, the centre of
    The magic circle there,
Was one whose being filled with love
    The breathless atmosphere….

PERCY BYSSHE SHELLEY
(1792-1822)

EVERYTHING IS PLUNDERED...

Everything is plundered, betrayed, sold,
Death's great black wing scrapes the air,
Misery gnaws to the bone.
Why then do we not despair?

By day, from the surrounding woods,
cherries blow summer into town;
at night the deep transparent skies
glitter with new galaxies.

And the miraculous comes so close
to the ruined, dirty houses —
something not known to anyone at all,
but wild in our breast for centuries.

ANNA AKHMATOVA (1889-1966)

A TOUCH OF THE ETERNAL

It was very early, and the wood was in a charmed stillness.... Amber shut her eyes, listening, not with the ear, but with the soul. Here, where the sounds of the world died away like a lapsing tide, she heard the sad rumour that life makes, stirring and murmuring in the silver hush of nonentity. She heard the moth-flicker of worlds slipping out into their age-long life, and their return – faint as the hum of a spent bee – to their everlastingly by mysterious cause.... Then a tremor of wind shook the flowering tree-tops, and she awoke again to the senses, to the strangeness of these utterances of the leaves. For the forest tree keeps in her heart secrets of days long gone – days when the little bruit of man was drowned by the infinite grave forest murmur.... Every tassel and streamer, every rosette, and cluster and catkin, all the minute, unnoticed bloom of the woodland, seemed to envelop her in scent and rustling music. Close about her she had the bloom of the wild fruit trees in the Birds' Orchard. It was steep and green as the hills in a dream, and up the slope, poised in attitudes of wind-blown grace, climbed a company of crab trees. Their brown and fissured trunks were lichened and mossy; their tops were broad, and low and rosy. Standing on the slope, Amber could see them, mushroom-like, spread with pink tapestry. She could see the burnished bees, tethered by desire, hovering in thousands, falling in and out of the rose-coloured cups. She was drenched in the scent which, although more delicate than that of an orchard tree, is not less heady – the scent of wild apple in the early sun. The pale flowers and the bright, close-fisted buds were packed layer upon layer in the exquisite freshness of romance. From the middle of a cup-shaped hollow rose a wild pear tree, forty feet high, flowering late on its windy hillside. It was white as a summer cloud, with its cymes of large, rose-like blossoms. Its scent, more unearthly than the apple, wandered down with the breezes that stole along the dazzling terraces. Amber loved pear blossom; she delighted in the creamy, nut-like buds, each with its cross of soft rose-colour, a little paler than the velvety stamens of the open flower, and contrasting delicately with the silver calyx.... But she could not linger by the pear tree; there were so many other things to see. She had the feeling, almost of greed, that such days bring – days with something glistening in them, a touch of the eternal. She felt like a child on the sea beach, loaded with shells veined with rainbow tints, pearly, fiery, and all with the sea in them....

She climbed to the buckthorn grove. There they stood, creating their own atmosphere, as do all groups of trees. They dwelt in green fire, for their leaves – thin as those of beeches – were young and fresh. Their stems were of regal purple. Their creamy flowers, long-stalked, five-petalled, sweet, starred the bases of the leaf clusters.... A breath of scented air came from the hilltops and stole among the branches. That which had form, and knew the mortality which is in form, trembled before that which passed, formless and immortal. It seemed content to linger here for a little while, before the momentary existence of this visible beauty slipped into nothingness; but it did not commit its whole self to any creature of matter, neither to dew-dark petal nor gold-eyed bird. It passed in the wood, as sunlight passes, or as the wind goes by, lifting the leaves with indifferent fingers, or like the rain stroking the flowers in childlike carelessness. Because of it the place became no mere congregation of trees, but a thing fierce as stellar space. Yet in the wood it never nested, never came homing to the spangled meadow. For it possesses itself for ever in a vitality withheld, immutable. It was this that drew Amber with breathless curiosity into the secret haunts of nature. It was this that struck her now into a kind of ecstasy....

MARY WEBB (1881-1927), FROM "THE HOUSE IN DORMER FOREST"

MARCH 13, 1842

Nature doth thus kindly heal every wound. By the mediation of a thousand little mosses and fungi, the most unsightly objects become radiant of beauty. There seem to be two sides of this world, presented us at different times, as we see things in growth or dissolution, in life or death. For seen with the eye of the

poet... all things are alive and beautiful; but seen with the historical eye, or eye of the memory, they are dead and offensive. If we see Nature as pausing, immediately all mortifies and decays; but seen as progressing, she is beautiful.

HENRY DAVID THOREAU (1817-1862)

PIUTE CREEK

One granite ridge
A tree, would be enough
Or even a rock, a small creek,
A bark shred in a pool.
Hill beyond hill, folded and twisted
Tough trees crammed
In thin stone fractures
A huge moon on it all, is too much.
The mind wanders. A million
Summers, night air still and the rocks
Warm. Sky over endless mountains.
All the junk that goes with being human
Drops away, hard rock wavers
Even the heavy present seems to fail
This bubble of a heart.
Words and books
Like a small creek off a high ledge
Gone in the dry air.

A clear, attentive mind
Has no meaning but that
Which sees is truly seen.
No one loves rock, yet we are here
Night chills. A flick
In the moonlight
Slips into Juniper shadow:
Back there unseen
Could proud eyes
Of Cougar or Coyote
Watch me rise and go.

GARY SNYDER, B. 1930

There is a pleasure in the pathless woods,

There is a rapture on the lonely shore,

There is society, where none intrudes,

By the deep Sea, and music in its roar:

O love not Man the less, but Nature more,

From these our interviews, in which I steal

For all I may be, or have been before,

To mingle with the Universe, and feel

What I can ne'er express, yet can not all conceal.

LORD BYRON (1788-1824), FROM "CHILDE HAROLD'S PILGRIMAGE"

SOME TREES

These are amazing: each
Joining a neighbor, as though speech
Were a still performance.
Arranging by chance

To meet as far this morning
From the world as agreeing
With it, you and I
Are suddenly what the trees try

To tell us we are:
That their merely being there
Means something; that soon
We may touch, love, explain.

And glad not to have invented
Such comeliness, we are surrounded:
A silence already filled with noises,
A canvas on which emerges

A chorus of smiles, a winter morning.
Placed in a puzzling light, and moving,
Our days put on such reticence
These accents seem their own defense.

JOHN ASHBERY, B. 1927

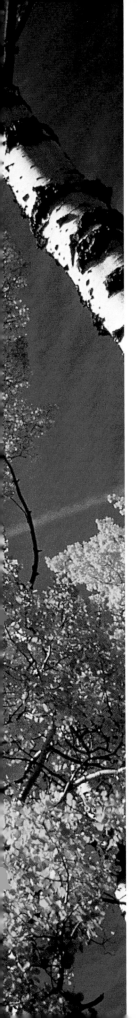

When we get out of the glass bottles of our ego,

and when we escape like squirrels turning in the

      cages of our personality

and get into the forests again,

we shall shiver with cold and fright

but things will happen to us

so that we don't know ourselves.

Cool, unlying life will rush in,

and passion will make our bodies taut with power,

we shall stamp our feet with new power

and old things will fall down,

we shall laugh, and institutions will curl up like

      burnt paper.

D . H . L A W R E N C E (1 8 8 5 - 1 9 3 0)

TO INSCRIBE ON A PICTURE OF A SKULL I PAINTED

All things born of causes end when causes run out;

but causes, what are they born of?

That very first cause — where did it come from?

At this point words fail me, workings of my mind go dead.

I took these words to the old woman in the house to the east;

the old woman in the house to the east was not pleased.

I questioned the old man in the house to the west;

the old man in the house to the west puckered his brow and walked away.

I tried writing the question on a biscuit, fed it to the dogs,

but even the dogs refused to bite....

RYOKAN (1758-1831)

The desert is the last place you can see all around you. The light out here makes everything close, and it is never, never the same. Sometimes the light hits the mountains from behind and front at the same time, and it gives them the look of Japanese prints, you know, distances in layers.

GEORGIA O'KEEFFE (1887-1986)

Rainbows for robes, wind for horses,

whirling whirling, the Lord of the Clouds comes down,

tigers twanging zithers, luan birds to turn his carriage,

and immortal men in files thick as hemp —

    Suddenly my soul shudders, my spirit leaps,

    in terror I rise up with repeated sighs;

    only the mat and pillow where now I woke —

    lost are the mists of a moment ago!

All the joys of the world are like this,

the many-evented past a river flowing east.

I leave you now — when will I return? —

to loose the white deer among green bluffs,

in my wandering to ride them in search of famed hills.

How can I knit brows, bend back to serve influence and power,

never dare to wear an open-hearted face?

LI PO (7 0 1 - 7 6 2)

LIFE ON COLD MOUNTAIN

I climb the road to Cold Mountain,
the road to Cold Mountain that never ends.
The valleys are long and strewn with boulders,
the streams broad and banked with thick grass.
Moss is slippery though no rain has fallen;
pines sigh but it isn't the wind.
Who can break from the snares of the world
and sit with me among the white clouds?

Cold Mountain is full of weird sights;
people who try to climb it always get scared.
When the moon shines, the water glints and sparkles;
when the wind blows, the grasses rustle and sigh.
Snowflakes make blossoms for the bare plum,
clouds in place of leaves for the naked trees.
At a touch of rain the whole mountain shimmers –
but only in good weather can you make the climb....

Among a thousand clouds and ten thousand streams
here lives an idle man,
in the daytime wandering over green mountains,
at night coming home to sleep by the cliff.
Swiftly the springs and autumns pass,
but my mind is at peace, free of dust and delusion.
How pleasant, to know I need nothing to lean on,
to be still as the waters of the autumn river!

My house is at the foot of the green cliff,
My garden, a jumble of weeds I no longer bother to mow.
New vines dangle in twisted strands
Over old rocks rising steep and high.
Monkeys make off with the mountain fruits,
The white heron crams his bill with fish from the pond,
While I, with a book or two of the immortals,
Read under the trees – mumble, mumble.

HAN SHAN (8TH CENTURY)

TALK IN THE MOUNTAINS

You ask me, "Why dwell among green mountains?"
I laugh in silence; my soul is quiet.
Peach blossom follows the moving water;
Here is a heaven and earth, beyond the world of men.

LI PO (701-762)

What message from imagined Paradise
Can bring hope to us, whose daily news
Is of polluted forests, poisoned seas,
Of the polluted air, the clouds
Laden with sour vapours from our furnaces,
What can we hope or pray for that can heal these
Mortal wounds of our brief beloved earth?
There is no turning, no returning
For us, whose birth
Sets time on the move, first cause
Of all this consequence.
Implicit in each beginning is its end:
What poet can write
Of beauty truth and goodness in these days
(Or say rather, of what else?).
Oh, I know it all as well as any,
And yet I feel delight
As I look up into today's blue skies
Where the sun still gives light
And warmth (wisdom and love, Blake says)
And on this doomed decaying city rise
On the last days as on the first
These marvels inexhaustible and boundless.

KATHLEEN RAINE, B.1908

YES TO THE EARTH

So radiant in certain mornings' light
With its roses and its cypress trees
Is Earth, or with its grain and olives;

So suddenly it is radiant on the soul,
Which stands then alone and forgetful
Though just a moment earlier the soul
Wept bloody tears or dwelt in bitterness;

So radiant in certain mornings' light
Is Earth, and in its silence so expressive,
This wondrous lump rolling in its skies;
Beautiful, tragic in solitude, yet smiling,

That the soul, unasked, replies
"Yes" replies, "Yes" to the Earth,
To the indifferent Earth, "Yes!",

Even though next instant skies
Should darken, roses too, and cypresses,
Or the effort of life grow heavier still,
The act of breathing even more heroic,

"Yes" replies the battered soul to Earth,
So radiant in the light of certain mornings
Beautiful above all things, and human hope.

SIBILLA ALERAMO (1876-1960)

ONE MAN CANNOT DO RIGHT IN ONE DEPARTMENT OF LIFE

WHILST HE IS OCCUPIED IN DOING WRONG IN ANY OTHER DEPARTMENT.

LIFE IS ONE INDIVISIBLE WHOLE.

MAHATMA GANDHI (1869-1948)

What is of all things most yielding
Can overcome that which is most hard,
Being substanceless, it can enter in
even where there is no crevice.
That is how I know the value
of action which is actionless.

But that there can be teaching without words,
Value in action which is actionless
Few indeed can understand.

LAO TZU (6TH CENTURY B.C.)

When moods come I follow them alone,

to no purpose learning fine things for myself,

going till I come to where the river ends,

sitting and watching when clouds rise up.

By chance I meet an old man of the woods;

we talk and laugh – we have no "going-home" time.

WANG WEI (699-759)

It is Spring on the lake and
I run six or seven miles.
Sunset, I notice a few
Houses. Children are driving
Home the ducks and geese. Young girls
Are coming home carrying
Mulberry leaves and hemp. Here
In this hidden village the
Old ways still go on. The crops
Are good. Everybody is
Laughing. This old man fastens
His boat and climbs up the bank.
Tipsy, he holds fast to the vines.

LU YU (1125-1209)

THE LEAF

"How beautifully it falls", you said,
As a leaf turned and twirled
On invisible wind upheld,
How airily to ground
Prolongs its flight.

You for a leaf-fall forgot
Old age, loneliness,
Body's weary frame,
Crippled hands, failing sense,
Unkind world and its pain.

What did that small leaf sign
To you, troth its gold
Plight 'twixt you and what unseen
Messenger to the heart
From a fair, simple land?

KATHLEEN RAINE, B. 1908

Though we travel the world over to find the beautiful,
we must carry it with us or we find it not.

ANONYMOUS

TEXT ACKNOWLEDGEMENTS

Exley Publications is very grateful for permission to reproduce copyright material. Whilst every reasonable effort has been made to trace copyright holders, we would be pleased to hear from any not here acknowledged. ANON (Eskimo): "Delight in Nature", from *Eskimo Poems from Canada and Greenland,* translated by Tom Lowenstein. Published by Allison and Busby, 1973, this translation © Tom Lowenstein. ANON (Medieval Latin): from "The Cambridge Songs", translated by Willis Barnstone from *The Book of Women Poets from Antiquity to Now* by Aliki and Willis Barnstone. © 1980 Schocken Books Inc. Used by permission of Schocken Books, distributed by Pantheon Books, a division of Random House Inc. ANNA AKHMATOVA: "A land not mine" translated by Jane Kenyon, © 1976. Permission granted by The Estate of Jane Kenyon. "Everything is Plundered" from *Selected Poems*. First published in the USA by Little, Brown in 1973, in the U.K. by Collins and Harvill Press 1974. © in the translations Stanley Kunitz and Max Hayward 1967, 1968, 1972, 1973. Reproduced by permission of The Harvill Press. SIBILLA ALERAMO: "Yes to The Earth", translated by Ivo Mosley from *The Green Book of Poetry*. Edited by Ivo Mosley, published by Frontier Publishing. © 1993 Ivo Mosley. JOHN ASHBERY: "Some Trees", by John Ashbery. (New Haven: Yale University Press, 1957) © 1957 by John Ashbery. Reprinted by permission of Georges Borchardt Inc for the author and Carcanet Press Limited. FRANCES BELLERBY: "Plash Mill, Under The Moor" from *The Selected Poems of Frances Bellerby,* published by Eritharmon Press. Reprinted by permission of David Higham Associates. THORKILD BJORNVIG: From "The Owl", translated by Robert Bly, from *News of the Universe - Poems of Twofold Consciousness* © 1980, 1995 Robert Bly. reprinted by permission of Sierra Club Books. WENDELL BERRY: "The Peace of Wild Things" from *Openings* © 1968 and renewed 1996 by Wendell Berry. Reprinted by permission of Harcourt, Brace and Company. RACHEL CARSON: From *The Edge of The Sea* published by Houghton Mifflin Co. © 1955 Rachel Carson, renewed 1983 by Roger Christie. Reprinted by permission of Penguin Books Ltd and Houghton Mifflin Co. All rights reserved. LAWRENCE COLLINS: From *Only a Little Planet* by David Bower and Lawrence Collins. Published by Herder and Herder. © Friends of the Earth, Inc. STEPHEN DUNN: "Underneath" from *Local Time,* published by Quill/William Morrow. © 1986 Stephen Dunn. Reprinted by permission of the author. HERMAN HESSE: "Sometimes", translated by Robert Bly, from *News of the Universe: Poems of Twofold Consciousness* © 1980, 1995 Robert Bly. Reprinted by permission of Sierra Club Books. RANDALL JARRELL: "Bats" from *The Bat Poet* published by Michael di Capua Books and HarperCollins Publishers © 1963, 1965 Randall Jarrell. Permission granted by Rhoda Weyr Agency, NY. D.H. LAWRENCE: From "Whales Not Weep! and Escape" from *The Complete Poems of D.H. Lawrence* edited by V de Sola Pinto & FW Roberts. © 1964, 1971 Angelo Ravagli and CM Weekley, Executors of the Estate of Frieda Lawrence Ravagli. Used by permission of Viking Penguin, a division of Penguin Putnam Inc. and Laurence Pollinger Ltd. DENISE LEVERTOV: "Come Into Animal Presence" from *Poems 1960-1967* by Denise Levertov, published by New Directions Publishing Co. © 1966 Denise Levertov. Reprinted by permission of New Directions Publishing Corp. and Laurence Pollinger Ltd. PETER LEVI: "In midwinter a wood was", from *Collected Poems 1955-1975,* published in 1984 by Anvil Press Poetry. CECIL DAY LEWIS: "Maple and Sumach", from *Complete Poems of C. Day Lewis 1925-1972.* Published by Sinclair-Stevenson (1992) © 1992 in this edition and the Estate of C. Day Lewis. JOE MILLER: From *Save The Earth* by Jonathon Porrit, published by Dorling Kindersley. © 1991 Jonathon Porrit and Dorling Kindersley. MARY OLIVER: "Wild Geese" from *Dream Work* by Mary Oliver. © 1986 by Mary Oliver. Reprinted by permission of Grove/Atlantic, Inc. "Some Questions You Might Ask" from *House of Light* © 1990 by Mary Oliver. Used by permission of Beacon Press, Boston. SHEENAGH PUGH: "After I came back from Iceland", from *Selected Poems.* © 1990 Sheenagh Pugh, published by Seren Books. KATHLEEN RAINE: "Vegetation", "What message from imagined Paradise...", "The Sphere", "Message from Home", and "The Leaf", from *Selected Poems,* © 1988 Kathleen Raine. Published by Golgonooza Press, reprinted by permission. "Heirloom", from *The Lost Country* © 1971 Kathleen Raine. Published by Allen and Unwin. "The very leaves of the Acacia-tree are London...", from *The Oval Portrait,* © 1977 Kathleen Raine. Published by Allen and Unwin. Used by permission of HarperCollins Ltd. MIRIAM ROTHSCHILD: From *Save The Earth* by Jonathon Porrit, published by Dorling Kindersley Ltd. © Jonathon Porrit. JALAL AD-DIN AR-RUMI: from *The Essential Rumi,* translated by John Moyne and Coleman Barks. © 1984 Threshold Books, 139 Main Street, Battleboro, VT 05301 USA. RYOKAN: From "To Inscribe on a Picture of a Skull I Painted", from *The Country of Eight Islands,* translated by Hiroaki Sato and Burton Watson. © 1981 by Hiroaki Sato and Burton Watson. Used by permission of Doubleday, a division of Bantam Doubleday Dell Publishing Group Inc. LAWRENCE SAIL: From *The Waterbuck,* © Lawrence Sail. Reprinted with permission of the author. HAN SHAN: "Life on Cold Mountain", from *Cold Mountain: 100 Poems by the T'ang Poet Han Shan* by Burtin Watson. Used by permission of Columbia University Press. GARY SNYDER: "Piute Creek", from *Rip Rap* by Gary Snyder, published by Grey Fox Press. © 1958, 1959, 1965 Gary Snyder. LEWIS THOMAS: "The World's Biggest Membrane" © 1971, 1972, 1973, by The Massachusetts Medical Society, from "The Lives of a Cell" by Lewis Thomas. Used by permission of Viking Penguin, a division of Penguin Putnam Inc. R.S. THOMAS: "Autumn on The Land", from *Song at The Years Turning,* published by Hart Davis. © 1955 R.S. Thomas. Used by permission of the author. JUDITH WRIGHT: "To Hafiz of Shiraz" from *Collected Poems 1942-1970,* published by Angus and Robertson. © 1971. Used by permission of HarperCollins Australia.

LIST OF ILLUSTRATIONS

Exley Publications is very grateful to the following individuals and organizations for permission to reproduce their pictures. Whilst all reasonable efforts have been made to clear copyright and acknowledge sources and artists, we would be happy to hear from any copyright holder who may have been omitted. Cover: © 1999 Jan Tove Johansson, *Dusk at the Bog, Aromassen, Sweden,* Planet Earth Pictures. Front endpapers: © 1999 Ivar Mjell, *Trees - Denmark,* Telegraph Colour Library. Title Page: © 1999 Jean-Pierre Pieuchot, *Boulders by Stream Gorge, Southern France,* The Image Bank. Pages 6/7: *Autumn Colours, Mountains, Snow, Oppland Norway,* The Image Bank. Pages 8/9: © 1999 David Jeffrey, *Earth in Space,* The Image Bank. Pages 10/11: © 1999 L. Hymans, *Wildflowers in Antelope Valley,* ZEFA. Pages 12/13: © 1999 Mauricio Abrev, *Mountains, Clouds and Sky - Serra de Estrella, Portugal,* The Image Bank. Pages 14: © 1999 Richard Exley, Private Collection. Pages 15: *Raindrops on Leaves,* ZEFA. Pages 16/17: *Ripples in water,* ZEFA. Pages 18/19: © 1999 Chuck Place, *Wild Iris cluster around the fallen trunk of an aspen in a large, open meadow, San Francisco Peaks, Arizona.* The Image Bank. Pages 20/21: © 1999 Joe Devenney, The Image Bank. Pages 22/23: © 1999 D. Noton, *Trees and Alps at Dawn, Garmisch Partenkirchen, Bavaria, Germany,* The Telegraph Colour Library. Pages 24/25: © 1999 Walter Bibikow, *Cordoba Pass, Argentina,* The Image Bank. Pages 26/27: © 1999 Joe Van Os, *Cuernos del Paine - Torres del Paine National Park, Chile,* The Image Bank. Pages 28/29: *Grass,* The Image Bank. Pages 30/31: © 1999 Pete Turner, The Image Bank. Pages 32/33: © 1999 Luis Padilla, *Field of Thistles at Sunset,* The Image Bank. Pages 34/35: © 1999 Eric Menola, The Image Bank. Pages 36/37: © 1999 Jean-Pierre Pieuchot, *North Island, New Zealand,* The Image Bank. Pages 38/39: © 1999 Don Landwehrle, *Yosemite National Park,* The Image Bank. Pages 40/41: © 1999 C. Molyneux, *North Wales,* The Image Bank. Pages 42/43: © 1999 B. Peterson, *Sunset through a window wet with rain,* ZEFA. Page 44: © 1999 Gerard Champlong, *Dawn,* The Image Bank. Page 45: *Eucalyptus branches, California,* ZEFA. Pages 46/47: *Penguins,* Telegraph Colour Library. Pages 48/49: © 1999 Don and Liysa King, *Backlit Cresting Ocean Wave,* The Image Bank. Pages 50/51: © 1999 Andy Caulfield, *Sea Turtle Swimming,* The Image Bank. Pages 52/53: *Humpback Whale,* Images Colour Library. Pages 54/55: © 1999 Tim Owen Edmunds, *Gulfoss Waterfall, Iceland,* The Image Bank. Pages 56/57: © 1999 Jurgen Vogt, *Chesterman Beach, Tofino, Canada,* The Image Bank. Pages 58/59: © 1999 Joanna McCarthy, *Waves rolling onto shore at sunrise,* The Image Bank. Page 60: © 1999 Michael Melford, *Chobe National Park, Botswana,* The Image Bank. Page 61: *Ivy,* ZEFA. Pages 62/63: © 1999 Colin N. Bell, *Scotland-Strathclyde-River Teith, Ben Ledi, Near Doune,* The Image Bank. Page 64: © 1999 Lionel Isy-Schwart, *Rocky Mountains National Park, Colorado, USA,* The Image Bank. Page 65: © 1999 J. H. Carmichael, *Scene on Hillborough River, North of Tampa, Florida,* The Image Bank. Page 66: *View over the Blue Mountains National Park,* ZEFA. Page 67: © 1999 Y. Miyazaki, *Underwater, Bali, Indonesia,* Telegraph Colour Library. Pages 68/69: © 1999 J. H. Carmichael, *Tropical Rainforest scene along the Napo River Eastern Ecuador,* The Image Bank. Pages 70/71: *Flinders Ranges National Park view in Aroona Valley, Australia,* ZEFA. Page 72: *Detail of butterfly wing,* Britstock-IFA/Breit. Page 73: *Earth View - Apollo 10 astronauts view of the Earth approximately 100,00 miles away,* Image Select. Page 74: *Earth and Moon in Space,* ZEFA. Page 75: © 1999 Phillip A. Harrington, *Diatom (unicellular algae),* The Image Bank. Pages 76/77: © 1999 Peter and Georgina Bowater, *River Lyon, Scotland,* The Image Bank. Page 78: © 1999 J. Marshall, *View of the goat rocks in winter,* ZEFA. Page 79: © 1999 Douglas Kirkland, *French Alps,* The Image Bank. Pages 80/81: *Deer in Winter,* ZEFA. Page 82: © 1999 Bullaty/Lomeo, *Maple Tree - Autumn, Massachusetts,* The Image Bank. Page 83: © 1999 Kaz Mori, *River and Fall foliage, Michigan,* The Image Bank. Page 84: *Snowy Owl (Nytea scandiaca),* ZEFA. Page 85: *Snowy Owl in flight,* ZEFA. Pages 86/87: *England Autumn Sunshine in Woods,* ZEFA. Pages 88/89: ©1999 David W. Hamilton, *Northern California,* The Image Bank. Pages 90/91: © 1999 Trevor Wood, *Winter UK,* Stockphotos. Pages 92/93: © 1999 Derek Redfearn, *Trees in Autumn colours, Wye Valley, Gwent,* The Image Bank. Pages 96/97: © 1999 H. Wendler, *Poppies, Organ Pipe, Arizona,* The Image Bank. Pages 98/99: *Dune primrose, Anza-Borrego Desert State Park, California,* The Image Bank. Pages 100/101: © 1999 Paul McCormick, *Grizzly Bear Family, Katmai National Park, Alaska,* The Image Bank. Page 102: © 1999 McCutcheon, *Weisskopfseeadler,* ZEFA. Page 103: © 1999 Frans Lanting, *Crimson Bee Eaters,* ZEFA. Pages 104/105: *Fruit Bat,* ZEFA. Pages 106/107: *Samburu: Waterbuck,* ZEFA. Pages 108/109: *Bluebells in Wood,* ZEFA. Pages 110/111: *Beech Tree,* ZEFA. Pages 112/113: © 1999 Lisa J. Goodman, *Wheat Fields, England,* The Image Bank. Pages 114/115: © 1999 Steve Satushek, *Punchbowl Falls, Columbia Gorge Area, Oregon,* The Image Bank. Pages 116/117: © 1999 Steve Satushek, *Denali National Park, Reflection Pond, Mount McKinley, Alaska,* The Image Bank. Pages 118/119: © 1999 M. Pedone, *Pine Forest, Italy,* The Image Bank. Pages 120/121: © 1999 Kalt, *Blossoming Cherry Tree,* ZEFA. Pages 122/123: *Blossoming Lime Tree,* ZEFA. Pages 124/125: © 1999 Dr. Mike Hill, *Leichens on Stone Wall, Skokholm Island, Pembrokeshire, Wales,* Telegraph Colour Library. Pages 126/127: © 1999 Andrea Pistolesi, *Tree on Mountainside, Sequoia National Park, California,* The Image Bank. Pages 128/129: © 1999 Brett Froomer, *Vancouver, Canada,* The Image Bank. Pages 130/131: *Aspen near Sonora Pass, Sierra Nevada Mountains, California,* The Image Bank. Pages 132/133: © 1999 Gill C. Kenny, *Aspen Trees, Green's Peak, Arizona,* The Image Bank. Page 134: © 1999 D. Muench, *Sand Dunes in the Rio Grand Valley,* ZEFA. Page 135: *Volcano, Hawaii Kilauea National Park,* ZEFA. Pages 136/137: *Huang Shan, China,* Telegraph Colour Library. Pages 138/139: *Spain, Picos de Europa,* ZEFA. Pages 140/141: *Autumn, Hunan, China,* The Image Bank. Pages 142/143: © 1999 Guido Alberto Rossi, *Piretrus,* The Image Bank. Pages 144/145: *Sunset at Bear Basin Pass, California,* ZEFA. Pages 146/147: © 1999 Vic Verlinden, *Scuba Diving,* Stockphotos Inc. Page 148: © 1999 Joe Van Os, *Spruce Forest and Pond, Afognak Island, Alaska,* The Image Bank. Page 149: © 1999 J.H. Carmichael, *Scene on Denny Creek near Snoqualmie Pass, Washington,* The Image Bank. Page 150: © 1999 K. Laubacher, *Stream,* Telegraph Colour Library. Page 151: © 1999 Chris Mellor, *Yangshuo Hills and Li River, China,* Telegraph Colour Library. Page 152/153: *Autumn Leaf on water,* Images Colour Library. Pages 154/155: © 1999 Bernard Roussel, *Country Landscape,* The Image Bank. Back endpapers: © 1999 Charles Weckler, *Palms on Beach at Sunrise,* The Image Bank.